# HAP...

# CONFIDENT

# CHILDREN

Believe Publishers
Email: editor@believepublishers.co.uk
Websites: www.desouza.tv
www.believepublishers.co.uk

Limits of Liability and Disclaimer of Warranty
The author and publisher shall not be liable for your misuse of this material. This book is strictly informational, educational and entertainment purposes.

Warning – Disclaimer
This training product is sold or provided subject to the condition that it shall not, by way of trade or otherwise, be lent, resold, hired out, or otherwise circulated without the publisher's prior consent in any form of binding or cover other than that in which it is published and without a similar condition including this condition being imposed on the subsequent purchaser. Requests for permission for further information should be addressed to the Author.

ISBN: 978-1-913030-32-2

# HAPPY CONFIDENT CHILDREN

## THE LIFE-CHANGING JOURNEY OF CHILDREN IN BRAZILIAN JIU-JITSU

### KATIE DE SOUZA

# CONTENTS

# INTRODUCTION

We are passionate about teaching children Brazilian Jiu-Jitsu. We understand that, at the core of every parent's heart, lies the desire for their children to grow into happy, healthy, and confident individuals.

It is agonising to witness your child in pain—whether that pain is inflicted through the torment of bullying, particularly if they are targeted due to their body size, or the quiet suffering they endure when they are overshadowed and overlooked because of their shy and reserved nature. It's incredibly difficult to see your child struggle with a lack of self-confidence, knowing the vibrant potential that lies within them.

In our journey through Brazilian Jiu-Jitsu, we have had the privilege of guiding a diverse range of children as they overcome significant challenges in their lives. We have been a source of support and mentorship for children who:

- Are living with autism
- Are managing ADHD
- Exhibit shyness or social anxiety
- Struggle with low self-esteem
- Engage in self-harm
- Have endured bullying

- Have exhibited bullying behaviours towards others
- Face behavioural issues or conflicts
- Lack focus and concentration skills
- Are working towards a healthier body weight
- Need help developing social skills

Through the disciplined yet compassionate framework of Brazilian Jiu-Jitsu, these children have discovered new paths toward growth, confidence, and positive life skills.

We have also had the joy of guiding children on their path to excellence. Among the young learners we have nurtured are those who:

- Already had a passion for sport and transformed into dedicated Jiu-Jitsu athletes
- Were naturally active and found a structured outlet to channel their energy while acquiring new skills
- Possessed a competitive spirit and sought to test their abilities through BJJ competitions
- Demonstrated a propensity for excelling in various sports

The teachings of Brazilian Jiu-Jitsu extend far beyond physical prowess. Through this martial art, we impart essential life skills to children, including:

- Persistence and resilience, teaching them to face challenges head-on
- Dedication to their craft and their personal growth

- Commitment to their goals and the practice of Jiu-Jitsu
- An understanding of how their attitude and behaviour shape their life outcomes
- Endurance and stamina, both physically and mentally
- The invaluable lessons that come from both victory and defeat—teaching them how to win with grace, lose with dignity, and continually learn from their experiences

This book aims to shed light on how Brazilian Jiu-Jitsu can be a transformative, empowering journey that nurtures your child's resilience, confidence, self-respect, and inner strength, equipping them with the life skills and tools they need to thrive.

# CHAPTER 1

## WHAT IS BJJ?

Brazilian Jiu-Jitsu is a martial art that originated in Brazil in the early 20th century. It is a martial art where the aim is to submit your opponent by arm locks, joint locks, and chokes.

BJJ is an excellent choice for parents who want to instil discipline, self-confidence, and practical self-defence skills in their children. Unlike many other martial arts, BJJ doesn't rely on brute strength or physical size to be effective. Instead, it promotes leverage, technique, and strategy will win against strength, so a smaller person can defend themselves against someone bigger, making it a great equaliser for kids of all sizes and abilities.

## UNDERSTANDING BRAZILIAN JIU-JITSU

Brazilian Jiu-Jitsu (BJJ) is a grappling, submission fighting which differs from other martial arts in several key ways. Unlike striking arts such as boxing or karate,

BJJ does not rely on punching or kicking techniques to defeat an opponent. Instead, it focuses on grappling techniques, such as joint locks and chokeholds, to subdue opponents. BJJ places a greater emphasis on positional control and leverage than many other martial arts.

The role of grappling and submissions is also central to BJJ. These techniques are designed to subdue an opponent without causing serious injury, making BJJ a highly effective self-defence system that can be used in real-world situations. By focusing on leverage, technique, and strategy, BJJ practitioners can control and subdue opponents without relying on brute force or aggression.

There are lots of different positions the children learn, both how to get into them and how to escape and get out of them.

# CHAPTER 2

## WHY BJJ IS GREAT FOR KIDS

### Physical fitness and coordination

BJJ offers many benefits for children. It improves physical fitness and coordination by engaging the entire body in a low-impact way. Unlike team sports that may require running or jumping, BJJ is focused on technique and strategy, making it a great choice for kids who may not enjoy traditional team sports.

BJJ requires children to use their entire body when executing techniques, which helps to develop their coordination and balance. As children practise BJJ techniques, they learn to move their bodies in new and complex ways, which can improve their overall physical coordination and motor skills.

BJJ techniques often require children to work with a partner to execute the technique effectively. This helps to develop their ability to anticipate and react to their partner's movements, which can improve their body awareness and coordination.

BJJ is a great choice for parents who want to help their children develop their physical fitness and coordination in a fun and engaging way. By practising BJJ, children can improve their overall health and well-being while developing important skills and attributes that will serve them well throughout their lives. It helps children to be active and stay fit.

## Persistence

With BJJ children will learn persistence. There will be times when they are unable to perform a certain technique or be able to do a certain drill. They may not be able to do even a roly poly but with persistence, they will eventually improve and be able to do the roly poly.

We had a young boy once who had a degenerative condition which meant he found it difficult to balance and walk as other children do. He walked on his toes to help himself get around. Although with this adversity he never let it discourage him from joining in with the other children and trying to do what they do. He joined the BJJ class and in the warmup, he would try and do the running like the others. To start he could only walk as he went around. And he got a little disheartened in himself until we explained to him that the more he practises and keeps on trying, the better he will become.

So he kept trying, sometimes losing his balance and falling over, however, he would get back up again and try again. He learnt the importance of being persistent. He is now able to run around with the other children in the warmup. His sense of achievement increased, and he became more confident in himself and believed in himself more as a result.

*Key point – Keep at it no matter what*

## Self-confidence

BJJ also builds self-confidence by teaching kids that they can defend themselves and control a situation, even against a larger opponent. This newfound confidence can translate to other areas of their lives, such as school and social situations.

BJJ can help children develop a greater sense of confidence and self-esteem by teaching them to overcome challenges and push themselves to their limits. Children who practise BJJ learn that they can achieve their goals through hard work and determination. As they develop their skills and progress through the belt system, they can take pride in their accomplishments and feel a greater sense of self-worth.

## Winning, losing and learning

It can be difficult for anyone to accept losing and not winning, especially children.

BJJ teaches children to look for the lessons they can learn when they lose rather than just getting upset.

There is a lot of sparring where the children are fighting each other, with the aim of winning by submitting their opponent or winning by points. There is never a draw in BJJ, someone must always win, even if it means the referee must choose a winner at the end. Because of this, each child will experience winning and losing.

I know in some schools they try to avoid children losing and being left out by creating certificates and awards for lots of different things so no child is isolated. In real life, however, sometimes you do lose, and things do not go your way. Learning to deal with that at an early age is a great advantage.

When a child loses their fight we encourage them to look and learn to see what they think they could have done differently. We give them feedback and support. We then work with them to improve their fighting skills or in some cases their confidence, to just try a submission or takedown in the first place, depending on what they need.

At the end of every fight, the children will shake hands and hug their opponent, congratulating them on their win. We teach children to be happy for their teammates and opponents' victories and not to be resentful.

Of course, this does not always happen with smiles on their faces. We've had children start crying when they lose, some have stamped their feet, but they are learning constantly. It takes time to develop their behaviour and skills and learn how to control their emotions and choose a different response.

We help children by example. Our head instructor competes internationally regularly all over the world. He does not always win, and he lets the children know that what he's learnt is that he will need to practise more and more and keep trying. Not to let a defeat get you down, that it's ok to be upset initially but then to focus on what you can learn and improve.

## TRAITS AND SKILLS DEVELOPED BY BJJ

However, BJJ is more than just a martial art; it is a way of life that can benefit children in many ways.

### *The mental benefits of practising BJJ*

BJJ requires focus, concentration, and mental agility. By practising BJJ children can improve their ability to concentrate and maintain focus, as well as develop mental resilience and toughness.

BJJ can help children learn to regulate their emotions and cope with stress, which can have a positive impact on their overall mental health and well-being.

### *Developing discipline through consistent training*

Consistent training is a key aspect of BJJ and can help children develop discipline and a strong work ethic. By attending classes regularly and practising techniques diligently, children can learn the importance of setting and achieving goals, as well as the value of hard work and perseverance. These skills can be applied not only to BJJ but also to other areas of their life, such as school, work, and personal relationships.

### Improving focus through mindful practice

BJJ requires a high degree of focus and attention to detail. By practising BJJ techniques mindfully, children can improve their ability to focus and concentrate, as well as develop their awareness of their own bodies and movements. This mindful practice can help children become more present and engaged in their daily lives, leading to greater happiness and fulfilment.

To develop discipline and focus through BJJ, children need to approach their training with a positive attitude and a willingness to learn. Encourage your child to set achievable goals, practice consistently, and be open to constructive feedback from their instructor and training partners. Remind your child to approach each training session with an open mind and a willingness to learn and grow.

BJJ can provide children with numerous mental benefits that can help them become more disciplined, focused, and resilient. By developing these skills through BJJ training, children can become better equipped to handle the challenges of life and pursue their goals with confidence and determination.

### Traits and skills developed by BJJ

Traits, skills, and behaviours can sometimes overlap, but generally, they can be categorised as follows:

### Traits (or Personal Qualities)

These are inherent characteristics that define a person's nature or disposition. They are often seen as innate or developed over a long period and are part of a person's personality.

Attitude - it refers to a person's general perspective on things and their manner of thinking or feeling about someone or something.

Behaviour - while specific behaviours are actions and can be changed or developed, a person's general behavioural tendencies or patterns can be viewed as traits.

### Skills

These are learned abilities. Skills are developed through training, education, and experience.

Endurance - while some might naturally have better endurance, it is also a skill that can be developed and improved with training.

Stamina - like endurance; while some may be naturally predisposed to have more stamina, it's also something that can be achieved through training and improvement.

These categorisations are not always absolute. For example, while persistence and dedication are generally seen as traits, they can also be developed and improved upon, much like skills. Similarly, endurance and stamina, while achievable through training, are also influenced by innate factors like genetics. Context matters too; in some situations, you might refer to stamina as an innate trait, while in others, you might emphasise the training aspect and call it a skill.

### Patience

Patience is a key life skill to learn early on, it's easy to get frustrated and want things to happen straight away, but that is rarely the case. Athletes who you see effortlessly performing techniques have been practising for years until it became second nature.

We reinforce the importance of patience when learning BJJ. We even have adults who arrive to start training and they want to know how fast they can achieve their next belt. It's not about speed or jumping belts quickly, it's about the journey. As in life, it's about the journey, not the destination.

It's about understanding, growing as a person, learning life skills, patience, determination, and sheer grit to see things through to the end no matter what. It's about developing a positive mental attitude and forming good habits and behaviours. These skills cannot be wished, they are developed and learnt over time, and this is where patience is your greatest virtue.

## Persistence

Brazilian Jiu-Jitsu is not just a martial art; it's a discipline that imparts invaluable life skills, one of the foremost being persistence. For children, BJJ provides an unparalleled environment to learn, understand, and internalise the essence of persistence through hands-on experiences.

From the very beginning, BJJ poses challenges that demand patience and tenacity. Children, when they start, might find themselves grappling with more experienced peers or facing techniques they cannot master immediately. Such instances, instead of becoming sources of frustration, transform into opportunities to learn persistence. Each time a child gets caught in a submission or finds themselves in a disadvantageous position, they are presented with a choice: to give up or to try again. Over time, the ethos of BJJ encourages them to choose the latter, fostering a never-give-up attitude.

Training sessions in BJJ also emphasise the value of consistent effort. Techniques in this martial art can be intricate and mastering them requires repeated practice. Children quickly realise that success in BJJ doesn't come overnight. Instead, it's a culmination of countless training hours, repeated drills, and learning from failures. This environment makes it clear that progress is a result of sustained effort and determination. Every small improvement becomes a testament to their persistence.

BJJ competitions and sparring sessions teach children to face adversity head-on. Whether it's an opponent who seems unbeatable or a technique that seems insurmountable, children learn to approach challenges with a mindset of perseverance. They come to understand that setbacks are merely stepping stones to success.

Brazilian Jiu-Jitsu offers children a tangible realm to experience and develop persistence. The mat becomes a microcosm of life, where challenges are met with resilience, setbacks with renewed determination, and successes are celebrated as fruits of persistent labour. As these children grow, they carry with them the indomitable spirit of persistence honed through BJJ, applying it in all facets of their lives.

### Dedication

Brazilian Jiu-Jitsu is not merely a physical discipline; it's an education in dedication. For children, BJJ offers a structured environment where the rewards of consistent commitment and unwavering focus become evident. As children navigate the world of BJJ, they come to recognise and value the importance of dedication.

Progression is marked by the colour of one's belt, and each promotion is a direct reflection of the student's dedication to the art. As children start as white belts, the journey to the next belt is neither quick nor easy. It involves hours of drilling techniques, refining skills, and understanding principles. This process imparts a crucial lesson: lasting achievements are not a result of sporadic efforts but of continuous dedication. Each time a child gets promoted to a higher belt, it reinforces their understanding of the correlation between dedication and progress.

The art of BJJ is intricate, with each technique having layers of complexity. While the basics might be easy to grasp, mastery demands unwavering dedication. Children learn that it's not enough to merely attend classes; they must be present mentally, observing, questioning, and practising consistently. The subtle nuances of a technique, like the precise positioning of a grip or the exact angle of a move, often become clear after repeated practice. Through BJJ, children understand that dedication means diving deep, refining, and revisiting until perfection (or something close to it) is achieved.

BJJ schools often foster a sense of community. As children watch their peers and instructors, they witness firsthand the results of dedication. Senior students executing flawless techniques, or instructors recounting tales of their early struggles and subsequent triumphs, serve as powerful testimonials to the magic of unwavering commitment. These stories and observations act as motivators, urging young learners to remain dedicated even when the path seems challenging.

Brazilian Jiu-Jitsu is more than a martial art for children; it's a lesson in dedication. Through its structured progression, intricate techniques, and the inspiring community, BJJ instils in young minds an appreciation for the power of dedication. As they immerse themselves in this world, they learn that in BJJ, and life, dedication is the key to unlocking true potential.

## Commitment

Brazilian Jiu-Jitsu serves as a masterclass in commitment. For children embarking on the BJJ journey, the mat becomes a transformative space where the principles and rewards of steadfast commitment are vividly demonstrated.

At the core of BJJ lies the emphasis on consistent practice and growth. Children, upon stepping into this world, quickly come to understand that sporadic engagement won't lead to progress. Instead, to truly grasp and master the myriad of techniques and strategies, one must show up, train, and engage regularly. Such a structure inherently teaches children the principle of commitment. Whether it's showing up for training even when they'd rather be elsewhere, or dedicating extra hours to perfect a challenging move, they learn that commitment is about making choices that align with long-term goals over short-term comforts or desires.

BJJ presents an environment where feedback is immediate and transparent. In sparring or rolling sessions, a lapse in commitment, be it in preparation, attention, or execution, is readily apparent. A half-hearted attempt or lack of focus can easily lead to an opponent gaining the upper hand. For children, these sessions become powerful lessons in the necessity of commitment. They realise that to succeed, both on the mat and off, commitment cannot be a mere afterthought; it must be at the forefront of one's efforts.

The grading system in BJJ further reinforces the importance of commitment. Advancing from one belt to another is not just about time spent but about demonstrable skills and understanding. This progression system underscores the idea that commitment is a holistic endeavour. It's not just about showing up but about being mentally, emotionally, and physically present and invested. When children earn a new belt, it's a tangible testament to their commitment, a symbol of the hours, days, and months they've dedicated to their BJJ journey.

Brazilian Jiu-Jitsu offers children a framework to understand, practice, and value commitment. Through its demanding yet rewarding structure, immediate feedback mechanism, and symbolic progression system, BJJ instils in young learners the profound realisation that true success, in any field, is a direct outcome of unwavering commitment.

Dedicated and committed are two terms that are often used interchangeably because they both suggest a strong sense of devotion or allegiance to a cause, task, or goal. However, there are nuanced differences between the two. Dedicated means someone might be dedicated to their craft, meaning they invest time, energy, and passion into honing their skills. Dedication often implies a personal connection or passion whereas commitment usually carries a sense of responsibility. When someone is committed to a cause, they feel obligated to see things through, even when challenges arise. BJJ fosters the development of both these attributes.

### How attitude and behaviour affect their life

Children's attitudes and behaviours play a crucial role in shaping their life trajectory. A positive attitude and constructive behaviour set the stage for academic success, healthy relationships, and overall well-being. Whereas, negative attitudes or maladaptive behaviours can hinder a child's social integration, academic achievements, and self-esteem. The way a child perceives challenges, interacts with peers, and responds to authority can greatly influence their experiences and opportunities.

Brazilian Jiu-Jitsu offers a transformative space for children to cultivate positive attitudes and behaviours. One of the foundational principles of BJJ is respect - for the instructor, for fellow practitioners, and for oneself. As children immerse themselves in this discipline, they learn the importance of listening attentively, following instructions, and treating others with kindness and consideration. This respect, cultivated on the mat, often translates to improved interactions with teachers, parents, and peers off the mat.

BJJ also challenges children's attitudes towards setbacks and failures. The nature of the sport ensures that no one wins all the time. This constant ebb and flow of success and failure teaches children resilience and perseverance. They learn to view challenges not as insurmountable obstacles but as opportunities for growth. Over time, the attitude of "I can't" morphs into "I'll try again." This growth mindset, fostered through BJJ, is invaluable in life, promoting tenacity in the face of academic, personal, or professional challenges.

BJJ provides an outlet for children to channel their energy constructively. For children who may be prone to aggressive or disruptive behaviours, the discipline and focus required in BJJ offer a means to harness that energy positively. They learn control, restraint, and the distinction between assertiveness and aggression. Through regular training, children often exhibit better impulse control, enhanced concentration, and a greater sense of responsibility.

Brazilian Jiu-Jitsu serves as a tool to mould children's attitudes and behaviours positively. Through its principles of respect, resilience, and restraint, BJJ equips children with attitudes and behaviours that set the foundation for a successful, harmonious life.

### Endurance

Endurance, both physical and mental, is a key component of personal growth and development. For children, cultivating endurance prepares them to face the challenges and rigours of life with resilience and determination. Brazilian Jiu-Jitsu stands out as a martial art that offers children a structured environment to develop and hone this critical skill.

Physically, BJJ training is demanding. From warm-ups to drilling techniques and sparring sessions, every element of a BJJ class pushes a child's stamina and cardiovascular capabilities. As they repetitively practise techniques, spar with peers, and work on their mat movement, children naturally build muscle endurance. The varied nature of the moves, ranging from defensive positions to attacks and escapes, ensures a full-body workout, enhancing overall physical stamina. Over time, as they train consistently, children can sustain longer bouts of physical exertion without tiring, not just in BJJ, but in other athletic and day-to-day activities as well.

Mental endurance is another aspect that BJJ uniquely addresses. The intricate nature of the martial art, with its countless techniques and strategies, requires a child to stay focused, even when they might be physically exhausted or mentally overwhelmed. Encountering a stronger or more skilled opponent on the mat, children often find themselves in challenging situations where giving up might seem like the easiest option. However, BJJ teaches them to persist, strategise, and adapt, fostering a mindset of endurance. They learn that, even in adverse situations, with determination and patience, they can find a way out or at least endure until an opportunity arises.

BJJ promotes endurance through its belt-ranking system. Progress in BJJ is slow, and advancements don't come quickly. This gradual progression teaches children the value of sustained effort over time. They comprehend that success, be it in martial arts or life, isn't about quick wins but enduring commitment.

Brazilian Jiu-Jitsu offers children more than just self-defence techniques; it provides a platform for developing endurance. Through its physically demanding training and mentally challenging scenarios, children learn the value of persistence, adaptation, and sustained effort, equipping them with a resilience that benefits them both on and off the mat.

### Stamina

Brazilian Jiu-Jitsu is more than just a form of martial art; it's a rigorous physical activity that demands and builds impressive stamina. For children, engaging in BJJ can significantly enhance their stamina, setting them up not only for success in the sport but also for various physical and mental challenges they may encounter in life.

From a physical perspective, a typical BJJ class pushes children beyond their comfort zones. The sessions start with warm-ups that include a mix of cardiovascular exercises and strength training, immediately challenging their energy reserves. When they proceed to the technical drills, learning and practising moves, they are continuously active, working various muscle groups. This consistent activity ensures that over time, their cardiovascular endurance improves, allowing them to sustain prolonged physical efforts without succumbing to fatigue.

Sparring or "rolling" in BJJ is where stamina truly gets tested. In these sessions, children engage in controlled combat with partners, trying to apply the techniques they've learned. Given the dynamic nature of these encounters, kids are in a state of constant movement - defending, attacking, and strategising. These intense bouts, which can last several minutes, compel the body to function efficiently under stress, thereby boosting both aerobic and anaerobic stamina. Over time, as children engage in more sparring sessions, their ability to handle prolonged periods of intense activity without tiring increases significantly.

Beyond the physical, BJJ also cultivates mental stamina. The sport is often likened to a game of human chess, where foresight, strategy, and patience play crucial roles. As children navigate the challenges of learning intricate moves, remembering sequences, and applying them in dynamic scenarios, their mental endurance is stretched. They learn to remain focused, calm, and analytical even when physically exhausted, translating to enhanced mental stamina.

Brazilian Jiu-Jitsu offers children an invaluable avenue to build stamina. Through its structured training sessions, intense sparring rounds, and strategic depth, kids not only develop the ability to sustain prolonged physical efforts but also enhance their mental endurance. This increased stamina serves them well in BJJ and proves beneficial in many other spheres of life, from sports to academic pursuits to everyday challenges.

### Difference between endurance and stamina

Endurance and stamina are terms often used interchangeably, but they have distinct nuances, especially in the context of sports science and physical fitness:

Endurance refers to the ability of an individual to sustain prolonged physical or mental activity over a longer duration. It's often associated with aerobic activities like marathon running, long-distance cycling, or swimming. When you think of endurance, consider how long one can maintain a particular activity.

Stamina is about the capacity to maintain consistent energy levels and power output for a short to moderate length of activity. It's more about intensity than duration.

Think of activities like sprinting or weightlifting, where you need high energy levels for a shorter period. When discussing stamina, you're often referring to the intensity one can manage and for how long.

If you were to consider a marathon runner and a sprinter, the former showcases remarkable endurance, while the latter exemplifies exceptional stamina. However, both concepts are intertwined in many activities. For instance, a soccer player might need the endurance to last the full 90 minutes of a match, but also the stamina to make intense, short bursts of speed or strength throughout the game. This goes for BJJ where you need to be able to last the full round and still have the explosiveness to do takedowns and submissions.

# CHAPTER 3

## INSIDE THE DOJO

In our academy, we have set up a training area called a 'Dojo' in an area which can be viewed by parents, who can sit mat side and watch. Dojo is the name of the matted area where they train.

Parents, grandparents, friends, and family love to be able to sit and watch their children learning and developing in BJJ.

We have found that this set up also helps the children as they can see their parents sitting watching them. This is more comforting for the younger children. However, it's also beneficial for the older ones as they love to be able to show what they can do to their parents. It means the parents can be more involved.

Our classes start with all the children entering the Dojo. As they step onto the mats they bow towards the mats and say 'Oss'. This is a sign of respect to the training area and to their instructor and fellow students.

Pronounced oss, like boss without saying the b.

# ORIGINS OF THE WORD OSS

The term "Oss" is believed to have originated in Japan, where it is used in various traditional martial arts, including Karate and Judo. There are a few theories about its exact origins:

### Theory 1

Oss is short for Onegai Shimasu. That "Oss" is a contraction of the phrase "Onegai Shimasu," which translates to "please teach me" or "let's train" in English. This phrase is used as a sign of respect towards a training partner or instructor.

### Theory 2

Derived from the word Osu (押す). It comes from the Japanese word "Osu," which means "to push." In this context, it may symbolise the determination and spirit required to push oneself to the limits during training.

### What Oss stands for

While "Oss" doesn't have a direct translation to English that captures its full meaning, it generally embodies the spirit of perseverance, determination, and mutual respect—values that are central to martial arts. It is a way of expressing a positive "fighting spirit."

### How Oss is used today

In modern times, "Oss" has become a customary term in Brazilian Jiu-Jitsu and various other martial arts around the world, not just those of Japanese origin. It is used in several different contexts, including:

As a Greeting - when entering or leaving the dojo (matted area), students often bow and say "Oss" as a sign of respect.

Acknowledging an Instruction - when a teacher demonstrates a technique, students may say "Oss" to indicate that they understand and are ready to try the technique themselves.

Before and After Sparring - it is common to say "Oss" to a sparring partner before and after a training session, as a sign of respect and sportsmanship.

To Show Respect to an Opponent - in competitions, athletes might say "Oss" to their opponents as a sign of respect before and after a match.

It's worth noting that while "Oss" is widely used and accepted in many martial arts communities, its usage can vary among academies and practitioners. Some embrace it wholeheartedly as a sign of respect and camaraderie, while others may use it less frequently or not at all.

# TYPICAL BJJ CLASS

Once all students have entered, they line up in order of their belt ranking, facing their instructor. Then the instructor and students bow towards each other whilst saying Oss.

## Warmup

A warmup then begins. During warm up the children will do some running, jumping, forward rolls, backward rolls, frog squats, skipping, hip escape moves, and drilling technique moves. Some moves they do will be part of a technique broken down into small parts, so they get their body used to moving in that way, warming up the muscles which will be used for fighting. These exercises are designed to prepare the body for the physical demands of BJJ and to prevent injury.

## Techniques

Once warmed up, the instructor will typically demonstrate and teach a specific technique or set of techniques. This instruction may include partner drills, where children work with a partner to practise the technique.

## Sparring

Following the technique part of the class, children will usually engage in sparring, where they practise the techniques they have learned in a more realistic setting. Sparring may be done with partners of similar or different skill levels and are supervised by an instructor to ensure safety.

The class ends with all the children lining up facing the instructor, the same way as when they started, bowing, and saying oss. They will then shake hands with each other in a line, thanking their teammates for their training, and then leave the matted area.

## Strength and grip training

At the core of our BJJ classes is to have fun, this is one of our main aims. Without fun, children do not learn as well, and they soon lose interest.

That's why some games and races are added to the classes. We have a climbing rope for children to practise their grip training and improve their strength. For them, they just see it as 'who can get to the top'. What they're really doing is developing the muscles in their hands so when they fight and must hold their opponent's gi, they have a strong grip to be able to control them and move or throw them where they want.

As part of the games and warmup, the children will learn various drills. These drills are part of techniques they will learn. The more they can automatically move their bodies in the correct way, the better, faster, and smoother their technique will be. They will develop muscle memory by repetition of moves, drills, and techniques.

## FULL BRAZILIAN EXPERIENCE

When we teach, we use the Portuguese words so they can fully experience Brazilian Jiu-Jitsu.

### Combate

Combate . . pronounced com..bat..chee

This is what the referee says at the beginning of a fight.

He raises his arm in the air between the 2 opponents and as he lowers his arm he says 'combate' literally translating to combat.

### Lute

During the fight, there may be a time when the referee places one of his hands on one of the opponents and says 'lute'. Or he may just point at the opponent if he can make eye contact with them.

Lute is pronounced loo..chee

Which means fight. This means he is giving that particular opponent a penalty and warning him to start fighting or he will be penalised again. This penalty is given when the referee perceives the opponent is stalling and not engaging in the fight for over 20 seconds. If the opponent continues to stall, a penalty will be given every 20 seconds, which could ultimately end in a disqualification.

## Parou

When the referee needs to stop the fight for whatever reason, he shouts 'parou' and holds both his arms out to his side at shoulder height.

Parou is pronounced par..row

And translates to 'stop'

The referee can say parou when the time has ended, when an opponent taps, or when an opponent's uniform has come undone and is causing an issue (eg their trousers have become loose and are falling down). The fight is then stopped for a few seconds for the opponent to redress themselves. They cannot use this time to recover so there is a maximum time limit to recompose yourself, 20 seconds to tie your trousers, 20 seconds to tie your belt and a further 20 seconds to tie the second belt if you are wearing the extra coloured belt, or you'll be penalised.

Another reason a referee shouts parou is when the fighters have got too close to the edge of the matted area. He stops the fight. Then moves the fighters back to the middle of the mats, then starts them (usually) in the same position.

## *Rules*

There are quite a few rules which we follow in BJJ. The rules were created by the IBJJF. The IBJJF rules are what we also use in the competitions we host.

The IBJJF rules also have a list of techniques which can and cannot be performed on different age groups and at different belt levels.

This is adhered to and was designed to keep the athletes safe from injury. Especially as children are still growing and developing. And the fact that the lower belt levels have less experience than those who are higher belts. It's all designed to look after the athletes the best way possible whilst ensuring they have the most fun and enjoyment.

Children are allowed to learn the following techniques:

- Takedowns – any
- Straight arm bars
- Americana
- Rear naked choke
- Cross lapel choke
- Triangle choke (no pulling head)
- Sweeps
- Guard passes
- Side control
- Knee on belly

- Back take
- Mount position
- Berimbolo

We teach the children how to defend and protect themselves. The best advice we give them though is to not engage in a fight in the street. Should they be attacked it's always best to escape and leave the situation and get help.

We teach Brazilian Jiu-Jitsu to be used in the Dojo. This is our primary reason for teaching, so they can become a fighter and compete.

We do not teach children to fight in the playground or anywhere outside the dojo.

Having a dojo for teenagers to come to after school, gives them something beneficial to do rather than wandering the streets bored.

We teach quite a few 11- to 15-year-olds. At that age we see their confidence soar as they become more comfortable to be themselves.

# CHAPTER 4

## HOW WE TEACH THE CHILDREN

This greatly depends on their age, natural ability, and how sporty and active they are already.

We do not set certain rigid rules for learning. Our focus for the children is to have fun and enjoy their time at Brazilian Jiu-Jitsu. If they don't enjoy it, they won't want to continue. If that happens, they will miss out on gaining all the life skills that BJJ has to offer. And we don't want that.

We want children to enjoy what they do. After all, every single one of us learns better when we're happy and doing something we enjoy. Our minds, when in a happy state, are open to receive.

We also teach through games and exercise. Climbing the rope is fun for the children, and they are improving their grip at the same time without realising it. They are also developing their strength. They play tug of war with a BJJ belt which is also improving their grip.

Younger children are still learning basic body movements, so we help them develop their motor coordination skills. They will start by learning roly polys, cartwheels, running, jumping, and skipping. This all helps with spatial awareness.

We teach children from 4 years old at our academy. We find that it is unfair to them to try and keep their attention if they are any younger. They are off wandering around because they are still too young to concentrate. All children vary greatly even within their own age group.

It's important to take your child's age and developmental stage into account when setting expectations for their progress in BJJ. Younger children may have a harder time with certain techniques or may not have the attention span to practise for long periods. Be patient and encourage your child to progress at their own pace.

BJJ classes are typically divided by skill level and age group to ensure that children are learning at an appropriate pace and in a safe and supportive environment. We have classes for three age groups: 4-6 years, 7-10 years, and 11-15 years. When children are 16 years old they usually train in the adult classes.

If your child has previous martial arts or sports experience, they may progress more quickly in BJJ. However, if they are new to martial arts or sports in general, it may take longer for them to develop the skills and techniques required for BJJ. Be sure to take your child's prior experience (or lack thereof) into account when setting expectations.

Every child has different physical abilities and limitations. Some children may be naturally more flexible or agile, while others may struggle with certain movements or positions. Be realistic about your child's physical abilities and encourage them to focus on developing their strengths while improving their weaknesses.

BJJ classes may also include additional components, such as competition training, strength training, or specialised training for specific techniques or situations. By understanding the structure of BJJ classes, you can help your child prepare for what to expect during each class and help them get the most out of their BJJ training.

Encourage your child to pay attention during instruction and to ask questions if they need clarification on a technique. Additionally, remind your child to practise good sportsmanship and to always respect their training partners and instructors.

The amount of time your child spends practising BJJ will have a direct impact on their progress. However, it's important to find a balance between practising enough to make progress and not burning out or becoming overwhelmed. Encourage your child to practise regularly but don't push them to practise for longer than they are comfortable with.

# GRADING - BELT SYSTEM

The belt system in BJJ is a way to measure progress and skill level. It's important to help your child understand that progress in BJJ takes time and that moving up the belt system is not an overnight process. **Encourage your child to focus on improving their technique and enjoying the process of learning rather than solely focusing on belt promotions.**

We follow the IBJJF belt grading system as a guide. Children will start as white belts. After approximately 2 months, if they have been attending regularly, and if they are starting to understand some of the basic techniques and can perform them, they will be awarded a white stripe on their belt by their instructor. The instructor will ultimately decide if they are ready to be graded or not.

All Jiu-Jitsu belts have a black tab near the end of the belt, this is where the stripes are added. Four white stripes will be collected over several months, then the fifth stripe will be a red stripe. The red stripe indicates that it is the last stripe for that belt, meaning that the next grading will be to go to a new belt. Once on a new belt, the collecting of stripes will start over again, four white stripes followed by one red stripe.

There are quite a few belt colours for the children to work through. This means they are graded more regularly than the adults, and this is to keep them more engaged and motivated to continue.

### Belts and their order

White, Grey/White, Grey, Grey/Black, Yellow/White, Yellow, Yellow/Black, Orange/White, Orange, Orange/Black, Green/White, Green, Green/Black.

By the time children reach age 16 they will no longer be on the children belt system, they will go onto the adult belt system. If by age 16 a child was on green/black belt, it would be up to the instructor as to whether they thought the child was ready to be graded to adult blue belt or whether they would go to adult white belt.

The main adult belts are:

White, Blue, Purple, Brown, Black

Adults collect 4 white stripes before moving belts, and it can take a new white belt anywhere from 2 years or more to reach blue belt.

## TOURNAMENTS

Tournament participation and competition can be an exciting and rewarding aspect of BJJ training for children. Here are some key considerations when it comes to tournament participation and competition:

### The benefits of tournament participation

Participating in BJJ tournaments can offer children the opportunity to challenge themselves, gain experience, and build confidence. Tournaments provide a chance for children to test their skills against new opponents and to apply the techniques they have learned in a competitive setting. Tournaments can help children learn important life skills such as sportsmanship, resilience, and grit.

### Understanding competition rules and regulations

It's important for both parents and children to understand the rules and regulations of BJJ tournaments. Rules can vary depending on the tournament and age group, but generally include guidelines on weight classes, time limits, and allowed techniques. Understanding the rules can help children prepare for competition and avoid disqualification.

### Preparing for competition

Preparation for a BJJ tournament should begin well in advance of the competition date. This can include practising specific techniques, increasing physical fitness and endurance, and developing mental toughness and resilience. It's important to ensure that your child is properly fuelled and hydrated before and during the tournament.

## Managing expectations and emotions during competition

Competition can be both exciting and nerve-wracking for children. It's important to help your child manage their expectations and emotions during competition. Encourage your child to focus on their performance and to avoid comparing themselves to others. Remind your child to breathe deeply and stay calm, and to approach the competition with a positive attitude and a willingness to learn and grow.

It's important to note that tournament participation and competition are not required in BJJ training. If your child is not interested in competing, that is perfectly fine. Encourage your child to pursue BJJ for their own personal growth and enjoyment.

We organise two main tournaments per year which are attended by over 500 people, children, teens, and adults. We also organise smaller events for the children only, where there are around 50 children in attendance. This is so the children can get used to the competitive environment on a smaller scale before advancing to the larger tournaments. We find it is a great entry into the competing world.

By understanding the benefits of tournament participation, the rules and regulations of competition, and how to prepare for and manage emotions during competition, you can help your child have a positive and rewarding experience with BJJ tournaments. Regardless of the outcome, tournament participation can offer valuable learning opportunities and help children develop important skills that can serve them well in all areas of their lives.

## EXAMPLES OF SOME TECHNIQUES

To watch videos of these techniques please visit www.desouza.tv

*Take down*

This can be by grabbing a single leg or by grabbing both their partner's legs and taking them away from them to lose their balance and fall to the ground.

*Counter for the Takedown*

Children are taught to stop their opponent from trying to grab their legs. They are taught to sprawl, therefore avoiding takedown.

The fight starts standing and then each opponent tries to take the other down, by doing a 'take down' move. This can either be a single-leg or a double-leg takedown.

Once the fight is on the ground, they are always seeking to gain a better position. After the takedown, they may land in side control.

### Scenario 1 – landing in side control

*Side Control*

They are holding their opponent on their side so they can't move. They have control of them from the side.

Next, they will want to advance to knee on belly, then onto full mount.

*Knee on Belly*

They will put one knee on their opponent's belly. Their opponent is lying on their back, and they will put one knee on their belly, and their other foot flat on the mat next to them.

From there they can go to full mount.

*Full mount*

They will now be across their opponent's chest, one knee on each side on the floor.

It's from here that they would want to go for a submission. They could go for a choke. Using their right hand to grab their opponent's right lapel and their left hand to grab their opponent's left lapel so their arms are crossed, they pull sideways, leaning forward over their opponent's head, putting pressure until they tap.

## Scenario 2 – landing one on top of the other

When landing, one person may land on top and one underneath.

The one underneath now has a chance to perform a sweep. This means switching their position, so they become on top. This is worth 2 points (so long as it's held for at least 3 seconds).

Different submissions can be performed from this position. One is the arm bar where you extend your opponent's arm and bend against the joint to inflict pain. All these submissions are applied gradually. You get the position and then increase the intensity, and when it gets too much for your opponent, they will tap. As they tap you let go of the submission.

They can tap using their hands, either on you or on the mat. Usually, you tap the opponent so they can feel you tapping. However, that's not always possible, so tapping the mat is fine. There can be rare occasions when both arms are trapped, in which case tapping can be done by using the foot or simply shouting stop.

In the case of children fighting, the referee will sometimes stop the fight even if the child has not tapped. The referee does that if they think the child will get hurt and cannot get out of the submission. It is done with the safety of the child in mind, even though sometimes the child and parent are upset afterwards. That is because the safety of the children competing is paramount. However, if an adult refuses to tap when a tight submission is on, the referee will not intervene often resulting in the adult getting injured.

*Submissions*

Chokes are another way of submitting your opponent. There are various types, but one is called 'The Rear Naked Choke' or its correct (Brazilian) name Mata Leao, which translates to 'kill lion'. Pronounced mah-tah lee-oun

We also call this the Baby Choke in our dojo, as it is the first choke we teach the young children.

You sit behind your opponent; you are on their back. You hook your feet in front of them around the inside of their legs. Then with your arms, you reach forward around their neck. You put one of your hands on the elbow pit or bicep of your other arm and then you fold that arm behind the opponent's neck. So you now have one forearm in front of their neck and the other one behind. You then squeeze to increase the pressure until your opponent taps.

This is one of the children's favourite chokes. Consequently, we often see them before or after class sneak attack their parents from behind and practise the choke on them. We hear a lot of giggles. After all, what children wouldn't want to play fight with their parents?

The main principles of BJJ include:

### Positional control

BJJ is based on the idea that if you can control your opponent's position, you can control the fight's outcome. This means that BJJ practitioners focus on gaining and maintaining dominant positions, such as side control, mount or back control, which allow them to control their opponent's movements and limit their options.

### Leverage

BJJ is designed to enable a smaller, weaker opponent to defeat a larger, stronger opponent using leverage. This means that BJJ techniques are designed to use an opponent's strength and momentum against them, rather than relying on brute force.

### Escapes and submissions

BJJ practitioners use a variety of techniques to escape from inferior positions and to apply submission holds that force their opponent to tap out. These submission holds include joint locks and chokeholds, which can be applied while standing or on the ground.

### Ground fighting

BJJ is primarily a ground fighting martial art, which means that practitioners focus on techniques that can be used when both fighters are on the ground. Ground fighting is an essential aspect of BJJ. Although fights start standing up, the aim is to take the fight to the ground and submit your opponent.

What's important to know about BJJ is that it's not just self-defence, or how to protect yourself. It is a sport and as such you want to win.

## POINTS AND SCORING

Submission is not the only way to win. You can win by points. Each technique which is successfully performed is awarded different points. A takedown is worth 2 points. For the points to count the opponent must stay on the ground for 3 seconds. If they manage to get up quickly after going down, then the points are not awarded and only an advantage is given.

To be awarded points you must hold the position for 3 seconds or more, otherwise you may only receive an advantage.

**2 Points:**
Take Down
Knee on Belly
Sweep

**3 Points:**
Guard Pass

**4 Points:**
Mount
Back Mount
Grabbing the Back

## Advantage:

The key word for scoring an advantage is 'almost.' Almost score a point. Almost get a submission. Awarded when position is not held long enough to be awarded points or when a submission was on but they did not tap and ended up escaping, you may get awarded with an advantage for attempted submission.

## Penalty:

Given when you are not fighting and instead are stalling the fight (for more than 20 seconds). Penalties can also be given for many other reasons, such as illegal grips and talking to the referee.

You can get 3 penalties then the 4th would result in disqualification.

First penalty just goes against you

Second penalty goes against you and your opponent is awarded an advantage

Third penalty goes against you and your opponent is awarded 2 points

Fourth penalty is a disqualification resulting in your opponent winning.

## Deciding The Winner:

The winner is the person with the most points, if no points have been awarded, or the points are equal, the advantages will be taken into consideration, and the person with the most advantages will win. Should the points and advantages be equal, then the person with the least penalties will win. Should the scoreboards be completely equal, then the referee will decide who should win, which is usually based on who was more active and offensive during the fight.

# CHAPTER 5

## ENCOURAGING YOUR CHILD TO PRACTICE

Developing a lifelong love for BJJ is an important aspect of ensuring that your child continues to enjoy and benefit from the martial art throughout their life. Here are some key ways to help your child develop a lifelong love for BJJ.

### Encouraging a love of learning

BJJ is a complex and dynamic martial art, and there is always something new to learn and explore. Encourage your child to approach their training with a love of learning and a curiosity about the art. Help your child set achievable goals and celebrate their progress along the way.

### Fostering a positive attitude towards challenges and setbacks

BJJ is not an easy martial art, and there will inevitably be challenges and setbacks along the way. It's important to help your child develop a positive attitude towards these challenges and setbacks, and to see them as opportunities for growth and learning. Encourage your child to approach challenges with resilience and determination, and to learn from setbacks rather than giving up.

### Creating a supportive and inclusive environment

BJJ should be a welcoming and inclusive environment for all children, regardless of their background, skill level, or physical abilities. Encourage your child to be supportive and respectful of their training partners and to treat others with kindness and empathy. Work with your child's instructor and dojo to create a supportive and inclusive environment where everyone feels welcome and valued.

### Encouraging participation in BJJ events and community

BJJ offers a vibrant and active community of practitioners, and there are numerous events and opportunities for children to get involved. Encourage your child to participate in local tournaments and to connect with other BJJ practitioners. By participating in the BJJ community, your child can develop a deeper love and appreciation for the martial art and the people who practise it.

By fostering a love of learning, developing a positive attitude towards challenges and setbacks, creating a supportive and inclusive environment, and encouraging participation in BJJ events and community, you can help your child develop a lifelong love for BJJ.

Remember, BJJ is a journey that requires dedication, discipline, and hard work, but it can also be a fun and rewarding activity that can benefit your child in numerous ways throughout their life. Encourage your child to approach BJJ with an open mind and a willingness to learn and grow, and to enjoy the process of discovering and exploring the art.

### *Parent Tip:*

Don't be harsh on your children. I've seen so many parents putting high expectations on their children, and so when their child loses, they feel really bad. When you put too much pressure on them to win, they get more stressed, and they feel like they will let you down. No child wants to let their parents down. They want their parents to be proud of them. I've seen parents shout at their children, tell them off for not performing well, for not trying a submission, for not being able to escape a certain position, or get that takedown, or whatever it is. And their child's face, energy, and self-esteem just plummets.

We want to teach children that it's okay to go after what they want and then fail. It may not work the first time, second or thirty-third time, but it's persistence, determination, effort, and attitude that make a difference. Keep trying, and keep putting in the effort. That's why we prefer to encourage and support the fact they are there trying again and again.

No one wants to do something and get told off for trying, it ends up demotivating them. Eventually, they will stop wanting to try because they will fear losing and being told off too much. They'd rather not take the risk.

We do not allow parents to coach their children when they are training and fighting because of the added pressure it puts on them. However sometimes straight afterwards they will tell them off once class has finished. We have spoken to parents to help show them an alternative way.

So what can you do instead?

Congratulate them on their efforts. Ask them how they felt their fight went. Ask what they think they could do differently.

Exercise – Teach children to look for the good. When they can identify for themselves something they have done well this ultimately boosts their confidence.

Sometimes as a parent, you have been supportive and haven't put any pressure or expectations on your child, but they have still put a lot of pressure on themselves.

So how do you deal with a child who is beating themselves up because they feel they were not good enough?

Teach your children to look for the good in what they did well.

There will be something they did that they could find, even if it was that they tried in the first place.

Ask your child first. It's tempting to try and flourish them with compliments and try to make them feel better, but the best way is if they can think for themselves and look at what they did to identify something they did well and felt proud of doing.

If they can't think of anything and they still feel like doom and gloom, ask them to tell you about another time or activity that they did well.

This is a good habit for them to learn and use. When they start to look for positive things they have achieved in their life they will become more confident and more willing to keep trying when faced with failure because they'll learn they are capable of doing things. They will not just learn they are capable rather they will 'believe' they are capable.

If people don't 'believe' they won't even attempt.

Regular practice is key to success in BJJ, and it's important to encourage your child to practise consistently and with dedication. Here are some ways to help your child develop a regular practice routine and stay motivated.

### Setting a regular practice schedule

Setting a regular practice schedule can help your child develop a habit of consistent practice. Work with your child to set a practice schedule that fits their schedule and allows for adequate time for rest and recovery. Encourage your child to stick to their practice schedule and to view it as a non-negotiable part of their routine.

### Making practice fun and engaging

BJJ can be a challenging and demanding martial art, but it can also be a fun and engaging activity for children. Look for ways to make practice more enjoyable, such as incorporating games or drills that focus on specific techniques. Encourage your child to practise with friends or family members to make the experience more social and interactive.

### Encouraging self-motivation and goal-setting

Developing self-motivation and goal-setting skills can help your child stay motivated and engaged in their BJJ practice. Encourage your child to set achievable goals and to track their progress over time. Help your child develop a sense of intrinsic motivation, where they feel a sense of satisfaction and enjoyment from the practice itself, rather than just from external rewards or recognition.

### Recognising and celebrating progress

Recognise and celebrate your child's progress along the way by encouraging your child to keep a training journal or log to track their progress and celebrate milestones such as belt promotions or successful tournament performances. Be sure to acknowledge your child's hard work and dedication and praise their efforts rather than just their accomplishments.

It's important to give praise to children for trying, not just achieving. Sometimes it will take a long time for a child to master a technique, or even a roly poly in the warm up, and if praise is only given once they can do that, it means they may be waiting a long time. And during that time their confidence may drop as they get frustrated with themselves that they can't yet get it right.

Whereas if you praise effort, this will lift your child's spirit, they will continue to keep trying, persevering and eventually succeed.

Praising effort shows your child you are observing how much they are trying. Children grow and develop in a positive environment. They need to learn it's okay to fail, they just need to keep trying again and again.

By setting a regular practice schedule, making practice fun and engaging, encouraging self-motivation and goal-setting, and recognising and celebrating progress, you can help your child develop a consistent and rewarding practice routine. BJJ is a long-term journey that requires patience, dedication, and a willingness to learn and grow. Encourage your child to approach their practice with a positive attitude and a love of learning, and to enjoy the process of discovering and exploring the art.

## Balancing BJJ with Other Activities

While BJJ can be a rewarding and beneficial activity for children, it's important to balance it with other activities and commitments. Here are some ways to help your child balance BJJ with other activities.

### The importance of balance and variety

Children need to have a balance of different activities and interests in their lives. Encourage your child to explore other sports or hobbies outside of BJJ, and to have a variety of physical and mental activities in their routine. This can help prevent burnout and ensure that your child is well-rounded and fulfilled.

### Setting realistic expectations

It's important to set realistic expectations for your child's involvement in BJJ, taking into account their other commitments and interests. Work with your child to set goals and priorities that are achievable and sustainable, and to communicate these with their instructors and coaches.

### Prioritising rest and recovery

Rest and recovery are important aspects of BJJ training, and it's important to prioritise them in your child's routine. Encourage your child to get adequate sleep, nutrition, and hydration, and to take breaks when needed. Work with your child's instructors and coaches to ensure that their training load is appropriate for their age and level of development.

### Communicating with coaches and instructors

It's important to communicate with your child's coaches and instructors about their other commitments and interests. Let them know if your child needs to miss practice for another activity, or if they need to adjust their training load for a particular week. Also work with coaches and instructors to ensure that they are aware of any injuries or health concerns that may affect your child's training.

By balancing BJJ with other activities, setting realistic expectations, prioritising rest and recovery, and communicating with coaches and instructors, you can help your child develop a healthy and sustainable routine that includes BJJ and other interests. BJJ is just one aspect of your child's life, and it's important to support their overall development and well-being through a variety of activities and experiences. Encourage your child to pursue their passions and interests, and to approach their BJJ training with balance, discipline, and joy.

# BEING AN ENGAGED AND SUPPORTIVE PARENT

As a parent, your role in your child's BJJ journey goes beyond simply driving them to and from practice. Here are some key ways to be an engaged and supportive parent.

### Understanding your child's goals and motivations

BJJ is a personal journey, and each child may have their own unique goals and motivations for pursuing the martial art. Take the time to understand your child's goals and motivations for practising BJJ and support them in pursuing these goals in a way that is meaningful and rewarding for them.

### Encouraging communication and feedback

Encourage open and honest communication with your child about their BJJ training. Ask them how they are feeling about their progress, if they have any concerns or questions, and how you can support them in their journey.

### Providing emotional support and encouragement

BJJ can be a challenging and demanding martial art, and your child may experience setbacks or frustrations along the way. Provide emotional support and encouragement to your child, reminding them of their progress and accomplishments, and encouraging them to persevere through challenges and setbacks.

### Recognising and celebrating your child's achievements

It's important to recognise and celebrate your child's achievements along the way. This can include celebrating belt promotions, tournament wins, or simply acknowledging their hard work and dedication. Recognising and celebrating achievements can help your child stay motivated and engaged in their BJJ journey.

By being an engaged and supportive parent, you can help your child have a positive and rewarding experience with BJJ. Your role as a parent is not to push your child to be the best or to achieve certain goals, but rather to support and encourage them in pursuing their own goals and passions. Encourage open and honest communication, provide emotional support and encouragement, and celebrate your child's achievements along the way. With your support and guidance, your child can have a fulfilling and enjoyable BJJ journey that will benefit them in numerous ways throughout their life.

# CHAPTER 6

## BJJ ETIQUETTE – ON AND OFF THE MATS

### *Respect at all times*

Respect is a cornerstone of Brazilian Jiu-Jitsu, as it is in many martial arts. Rooted deeply in its traditions, teachings, and interactions, the principle of respect in BJJ transcends mere politeness; it shapes the essence of the discipline, guiding both its practitioners and the environment in which they train. Emphasising respect within BJJ is essential not just for the smooth functioning of the dojo, but for the holistic development of its participants.

At its most basic, respect in BJJ is evident in the rituals and etiquette that frame each class. The act of bowing when entering or exiting the mat, or the gesture of tapping to signal submission, are symbolic of mutual respect. These acts acknowledge the shared journey of learning and growth, recognising the worth and dignity of every individual, regardless of rank or experience.

This culture of respect ensures the safety and well-being of practitioners. BJJ involves intense, close-quarter combat where the line between control and injury is thin. Trusting that one's training partner will respect boundaries and not intentionally cause harm allows for genuine engagement without fear. When respect underpins interactions, practitioners can push their limits, learn, and refine techniques in an environment where the intention is always constructive, never destructive.

Respect in BJJ extends beyond person-to-person interactions. It encompasses a love for the art itself. This means acknowledging the history, the lineage, the masters who've come before, and the lessons they've passed down. For a student, respecting their instructor by listening attentively, asking for permission before leaving the mat, or wearing a clean Gi are all ways of honouring the tradition and depth of BJJ.

Perhaps one of the most profound aspects of respect in BJJ is its capacity to shape character. As practitioners advance in their journey, they often find that the respect they cultivate within the dojo begins to influence their interactions outside of it. This tenet, central to BJJ, moulds individuals who approach challenges, relationships, and diverse life situations with humility, understanding, and a deep-seated admiration for the shared human experience.

While techniques, strategies, and physical prowess are integral to Brazilian Jiu-Jitsu, it's the ethos of respect that remains its beating heart. By emphasising and upholding this principle, BJJ not only nurtures skilled martial artists but also individuals grounded in empathy, humility, and genuine respect for others and the world around them.

## Teeth

Maintaining clean teeth before participating in Brazilian Jiu-Jitsu training isn't only a matter of personal hygiene; it's also a sign of respect, promotes health, and enhances the overall training experience for everyone involved.

Firstly, BJJ is a close-contact martial art, where practitioners often find themselves in very close proximity to their training partners. In such situations, maintaining fresh breath by way of clean teeth becomes a courteous gesture. No one wants to spar or drill techniques with someone who has poor oral hygiene. By ensuring clean teeth, practitioners show respect for their training partners, acknowledging the intimate nature of the sport and ensuring the comfort of others.

Oral health can directly influence one's overall health. Neglecting to clean your teeth can lead to the build-up of harmful bacteria which, if left unchecked, can contribute to oral infections, gum disease, or even tooth loss. Engaging in strenuous activities like BJJ with existing oral issues can exacerbate problems, particularly if one receives an inadvertent strike to the mouth or if the gum becomes irritated due to constant friction.

Having clean teeth can be a boost to one's confidence during training. Feeling fresh and hygienic can contribute positively to one's mental state, ensuring that the practitioner is fully present and not distracted by potential self-consciousness or discomfort. This mental clarity can enhance focus on techniques and strategies, making the training session more productive.

It's essential to recognise that gyms and dojos often foster community environments. Setting a standard of cleanliness and hygiene, including maintaining clean teeth, creates a precedent for all members. It promotes a culture of care, respect, and mutual consideration, ensuring that everyone can train in a comfortable and hygienic environment.

The simple act of ensuring clean teeth before engaging in Brazilian Jiu-Jitsu training can have a ripple effect, enhancing personal health, showing respect for training partners, boosting confidence, and contributing positively to the overall training environment.

## Hygiene

Cleanliness and good hygiene are paramount in the realm of Brazilian Jiu-Jitsu due to the close-contact nature of the sport. Prioritising hygiene before stepping onto the mat is not merely a personal responsibility; it plays a vital role in maintaining a healthy and respectful training environment for everyone involved.

To begin with, BJJ involves a significant amount of grappling, which brings practitioners into close physical contact with each other. This proximity can easily lead to the transmission of bacteria, fungi, and other pathogens. In the world of martial arts, skin conditions like ringworm, staph infections, or athlete's foot are notorious. Ensuring personal cleanliness dramatically reduces the risk of acquiring or transmitting these infections. It's not just about protecting oneself but about safeguarding the health of the entire gym community.

Being clean and maintaining good hygiene is a mark of respect towards your training partners. Turning up fresh, in a clean gi is a gesture that signals respect for the time and space of fellow practitioners. No one wants to roll with someone who has a strong odour or visible dirt, as it can be off-putting and make the training experience uncomfortable. By keeping oneself clean, a practitioner fosters an environment where everyone can focus on honing their skills rather than being distracted by hygiene concerns.

### Washing the Gi

Cleanliness extends beyond just the individual. It's about the uniform as well. Regularly washing and sanitising training attire and equipment, like gis, rashguards, and mouthguards, ensures they remain free from harmful microbes. This diligence helps in prolonging the life of the uniform and ensuring safety for the wearer and their training partners.

Cleanliness and hygiene play a psychological role. Being clean and feeling fresh can boost a practitioner's confidence and mental state. Instead of being self-conscious about body odour or potential hygiene-related distractions, they can focus wholly on their techniques, strategies, and the flow of the roll.

Maintaining cleanliness and good hygiene in Brazilian Jiu-Jitsu is a blend of self-care, respect for others, and the preservation of a conducive training environment. It ensures that practitioners can train effectively, safely, and harmoniously, fostering a culture of mutual respect and continuous growth.

Gis should be washed after each use. They can be machine-washed at 30 or 40 degrees. Remove from the machine and reshape then hang up to dry, do not tumble dry, otherwise, they will shrink. Belts do not need to be washed.

### Hands and Feet

Hands and feet should be clean before stepping on the matted area. We ask all children to wash their hands before starting class. If they have been to the beach or played barefoot outside then they must wash their feet too before stepping onto the mats.

### Short trimmed nails

Trimming one's fingernails and toenails might seem like a small detail, but in the intricate world of Brazilian Jiu-Jitsu, it's of paramount importance. Keeping nails short and neat is not just a matter of personal grooming; it plays a direct role in ensuring the safety and comfort of both the practitioner and their training partners.

The grappling-centric nature of BJJ involves various holds, chokes, and grips. With long or jagged nails, there's a heightened risk of accidentally scratching or cutting a training partner during these manoeuvres. Such injuries, though they might seem minor, can be painful and lead to more significant complications if they become infected. In the tight-knit, physical environment of a BJJ class, even a small scratch can become a portal for bacterial or fungal infections.

BJJ often entails complex ground manoeuvres and transitions. In the heat of a roll or spar, it's not uncommon for one's fingers or toes to get caught in the gi, mats, or even between the limbs of a training partner. Longer nails are more susceptible to getting snagged and might lead to painful nail tears or even full avulsions. Such injuries can be debilitating, causing a practitioner to miss significant training time and potentially lead to longer-term sensitivity or damage.

For the practitioners themselves, maintaining trimmed nails is also crucial for optimal grip and technique application. Long fingernails can impede one's ability to get a proper hold on their opponent's gi or body, affecting the effectiveness of their techniques. Over time, this can become a hindrance to technical growth and mastery.

There's a component of mutual respect in this practice. By keeping one's nails trimmed, a practitioner communicates to their partners that they prioritise safety and hygiene, respecting the shared space and collective health of the dojo. This act reinforces a sense of community and shared responsibility, foundational values in many martial arts disciplines.

The act of regularly trimming one's nails for Brazilian Jiu-Jitsu is a blend of self-preservation, safeguarding others, and upholding the values of the sport. It ensures a safer environment for learning, growth, and the enjoyment of the art.

### No makeup or piercings

Brazilian Jiu-Jitsu is a discipline that requires a degree of purity in approach, not just in technique but also in preparation. For children and teens, especially, it's crucial to understand that the BJJ mat isn't just a place of physical exertion but also one of respect, safety, and focus. As such, refraining from wearing makeup, face paint, or piercings during training sessions plays into these principles.

First and foremost, BJJ is a contact sport that involves close-quarters grappling. Wearing makeup or face paint can result in smearing, potentially obscuring vision or causing skin irritations. As partners grapple, sweat and friction can cause the makeup to transfer, which can be unhygienic and uncomfortable for both parties. Certain makeup products might contain chemicals or ingredients that, when mixed with sweat, might irritate sensitive skin or eyes. This not only poses a distraction but also can hinder the learning process.

Face paint, often used for events or celebrations, can have similar issues. Its thicker consistency can easily transfer onto gis, rashguards, or even the mats, creating additional cleaning challenges and potential skin irritation concerns for others.

Piercings present a more immediate danger. During the dynamic movements and holds of BJJ, there's a significant risk of piercings getting caught, tugged, or entangled in clothing, hair, or even an opponent's skin. Such incidents can lead to painful injuries, torn skin, or even more severe complications that require medical attention. Even piercings that seem secure or flush against the skin pose risks, as the pressure from holds or grips might cause discomfort or internal injuries.

Stepping onto the BJJ mat is a gesture of commitment to the art and to the shared experience with training partners. Coming prepared, without makeup or adornments, signals a level of respect for the practice, the instructor, and fellow students. It conveys a message that the individual is there to learn, grow, and immerse themselves fully without distractions.

While makeup, face paint, and piercings are forms of self-expression appreciated in many settings, the BJJ mat demands a different kind of preparation and respect. For children and teens, understanding and adhering to these norms is part of their holistic education in the discipline, teaching them about safety, focus, and the shared responsibilities of a communal learning environment.

### Shoes policy

### No Shoes on the mats

Every aspect of the dojo, from the techniques taught to the cleanliness of the mats, is treated with respect and care. The practice of ensuring that only bare feet tread upon the matted area is more than just a convention; it is rooted in safety, hygiene, and respect. For parents and their young martial artists, understanding the importance of this rule can enhance the training experience and foster a deeper appreciation for the discipline.

At the forefront is the issue of hygiene. Mats are the primary surfaces where practitioners roll, spar, and perform techniques. They come into direct contact with bare skin, faces, and open pores. Shoes, which travel outdoors and in public spaces, can carry a host of dirt, bacteria, and other undesirable particles. Introducing these contaminants onto the mat can quickly turn the training environment into a breeding ground for germs and potential skin infections like ringworm or staph. Especially in a sport like BJJ, where close contact is the norm, maintaining the purity of the mats is paramount for the health of all involved.

No one should walk on the matted area with shoes on, not even if it is momentarily for a few steps. Shoes must always be removed before stepping foot on the matted area. Even anyone sitting close by to the mats must not place their shoes resting on the edge of the matted area. Shoes must be removed first.

There's a symbolic significance to stepping onto the BJJ mat barefoot. It's a gesture that signifies respect for the art, the instructor, the dojo, and fellow students. By ensuring feet are clean and unshod, students convey their readiness to engage with the discipline fully, undistracted by external elements. It's a ritual that, especially for children, instils discipline and an understanding of the sanctity of the training space.

### Wear shoes whilst off the mats

However, while the matted area is a shoe-free zone, the areas surrounding it are not. Wearing shoes outside the mat is crucial to avoid picking up and transferring unwanted debris or contaminants onto the matted area. Parents can play a pivotal role in instilling this discipline in their children by leading by example and reinforcing the importance of these practices.

As mentioned, shoes must be worn at all times when not on the matted area, and when going to the toilet. We recommend using flip flops in the dojo as these are easy to slip on and off, as, and when you step on and off the mats. Always keep your shoes or flip-flops on until the last minute, then remove them just before you step onto the mats.

The simple act of removing shoes before stepping onto the BJJ mat symbolises a commitment to hygiene, safety, and respect. For parents and children alike, adhering to this practice can enhance the learning experience, ensuring that the dojo remains a clean, safe, and respected space for all.

### Food and Drink

Children may need snacks if they have come to training straight after school and are hungry. In this case, children must sit down to consume their snacks, preferably at the table, and certainly not to run around, nor eat on the matted area. All snacks should be eaten at least 30 minutes before their class starts to avoid feeling sick when they start their warm up.

This is the same for water intake. We advise small sips immediately before class rather than gulps of water, as this too will make them feel sick when running around.

No chewing gum or sticky sweets should be taken into the dojo.

# CHAPTER 7

## GETTING STARTED ON THE BJJ JOURNEY

Getting started on the BJJ journey can be both exciting and intimidating. If you or your child are feeling hesitant about beginning the journey, here are some ways to overcome fear and self-doubt and take the first step.

### Overcoming fear and self-doubt

It's normal to feel nervous or anxious about trying something new, especially a physical activity like BJJ. However, it's important to recognise that these fears and doubts are often unfounded and that the rewards of trying something new can far outweigh the risks. Encourage yourself or your child to face these fears head-on and to take the first step towards trying BJJ.

### Setting achievable goals

Setting achievable goals can help you or your child stay motivated and engaged in the BJJ journey. Start with small, attainable goals such as attending one practice a week or learning a new technique and build from there. Celebrate each accomplishment along the way, no matter how small.

### Embracing the learning process

BJJ is a journey that requires dedication, discipline, and a willingness to learn and grow. Embrace the learning process and enjoy the journey, rather than just focusing on the end result. Remember that progress and growth come from making mistakes and learning from them, so don't be afraid to try new things and take risks.

### Finding a supportive community

Finding a supportive community can make all the difference in your BJJ journey. Look for a gym or club that has a welcoming and inclusive environment, and that prioritises safety and respect for all members. Connect with other BJJ practitioners online or in person to build a community of support and encouragement.

By overcoming fear and self-doubt, setting achievable goals, embracing the learning process, and finding a supportive community, you or your child can take the first step on the BJJ journey. Remember, BJJ is a journey that requires dedication, discipline, and hard work, but it can also be a fun and rewarding activity that can benefit you or your child in numerous ways throughout your life. Encourage yourself or your child to take that first step, and to approach the journey with an open mind and a willingness to learn and grow. With time, patience, and dedication, you or your child can develop a lifelong love for BJJ and reap the many benefits it has to offer.

Here is our favourite quote from Zig Ziglar about getting started, which we also display in our dojo.

*"You don't have to be great to get started,*
*but you have to get started to be great"*

# GLOSSARY

**Armbar** a submission technique targeting the elbow joint.

**Baby Choke** our name for the Rear Naked Choke, as it is the first submission we teach the younger children, and we created a shorter name to use. It is a submission technique where you choke your opponent from behind by wrapping your arms around their neck.

**Belt Ranks** indicate the practitioner's level of skill. The children's belt progression is typically white, grey/white, grey, grey/black, yellow/white, yellow, yellow/black, orange/white, orange, orange/black, green/white, green, green/black. At age 16 children move to the adult belts, which are white, blue, purple, brown, and black. Some schools also have coral and red belts for very high-ranking practitioners.

**BJJ** is an abbreviation for Brazilian Jiu-Jitsu.

**Closed Guard** when the person on the bottom wraps their legs around the opponent's waist, locking their feet together.

**Combate** is spoken by the referee at the beginning of the fight. It translates to combat and means to start fighting. Pronounced com-bat-chee

**Drill** repeatedly practising a technique to refine and perfect it.

**Escape** a technique to get out of an undesirable position or submission.

**Gi** is the traditional uniform worn by practitioners. It consists of a jacket, trousers, and a belt. (Pronounced gee)

**Guard** a position where one person is on their back using their legs to control and defend against their opponent.

**Guard Pass** a technique used to get past the opponent's legs and secure a more dominant position.

**Half Guard** a position where one person controls one of their opponent's legs between their own legs.

**Hip Escapes** a fundamental movement in BJJ where one uses their hips and legs to move or create space.

**Kimura** a shoulder lock submission named after the judoka Masahiko Kimura.

**Mount** a dominant position where one person sits atop their opponent's chest.

**Open Guard** any guard where the legs are not locked around the opponent. Variations include spider guard, butterfly guard, and De La Riva guard, among others.

**Oss** is spoken as a greeting to other athletes, teammates or opponents. It is a sign of respect. It is spoken as you step onto the matted area, and spoken to your instructor and fellow teammates at the beginning and end of class, usually whilst bowing.

Pronounced oss, like boss without saying the b

**Parou** is spoken by the referee to stop the fight. It translates to stop. This command can also be given during the fight for them to pause and reposition. It is always given at the end. Fighters must immediately stop fighting when they hear the word Parou.

Pronounced pa-ro(w)

**Rear Naked Choke (RNC)** a submission technique where you choke your opponent from behind by wrapping your arms around their neck.

**Rolling** sparring or practising techniques with a partner.

**Side Control** a dominant position where one person is perpendicular to their opponent, controlling them from the side.

**Submission** a technique that forces the opponent to tap out, either due to pain or the risk of injury.

**Sweep** a technique, when guard exists, that reverses positions, typically moving from a bottom position to a top position.

**Takedown** a technique used to bring the opponent from standing to the ground.

**Tap** physically tapping the opponent, oneself, or the ground to indicate surrender or to signal a submission.

**Triangle Choke** a choke performed with the legs, trapping the opponent's head and one arm between the thighs.

# FINAL THOUGHTS

BJJ offers a wide range of benefits for children, both in terms of their physical and mental well-being, as well as their character development and life skills. Here is a brief summary of the key benefits of Brazilian Jiu Jitsu for children.

### Physical benefits

BJJ is a full-body workout that can help children improve their strength, flexibility, balance, coordination, and cardiovascular health. Brazilian Jiu Jitsu helps children develop their reflexes, agility, and spatial awareness, which can benefit them in other sports and activities.

### Mental and emotional benefits

BJJ can help children develop important mental and emotional skills such as focus, discipline, confidence, and resilience. The practice of BJJ requires children to be present in the moment, to think critically, and to learn from their mistakes. BJJ can help children manage stress and anxiety and can provide a healthy outlet for their energy and emotions.

### Life skills and character development

Finally, BJJ can help children develop important life skills and character traits such as sportsmanship, respect, humility, and determination. The practice of BJJ requires children to work with others, communicate effectively, and persevere through challenges and setbacks. These skills can benefit children in all areas of their lives, from school and work to personal relationships and beyond.

By understanding the physical, mental, and emotional benefits of BJJ, as well as the life skills and character development opportunities it offers, you can help your child have a positive and rewarding experience with this martial art. Encourage your child to approach their BJJ practice with a love of learning and a willingness to grow, and to enjoy the process of discovering and exploring the art. With your support and guidance, your child can develop a lifelong love for BJJ and reap the many benefits it has to offer.

### Next steps

We would love to help your children and guide them through their BJJ journey. If you do not live near one of our academies, then please look up BJJ in your area. Or get in contact with us for recommendations as we know a lot of good academies in the UK and around the world, and we can point you in the right direction.

# CONFIDENCE

*"The best gift you can give your child"*

**Book your child's taster today.**

**www.desouza.tv**

# BRAZILIAN JIU-JITSU

Give your child the gift of confidence, leadership, respect, focus & discipline with our Kids Brazilian Jiu-Jitsu classes.

**www.desouza.tv**

# KIDS BJJ JOURNAL

As referenced in the book it is a good idea to record your child's BJJ progression and training. We have designed a BJJ journal for children where they can write down what they have learned in their class, keep a record of their belt progression, and record the competitions they have entered and medals they have won. A place to record all their achievements and document all their proud moments in their BJJ journey.

Visit **www.desouza.tv** to get your **Kids BJJ Journal**

What a journey our boys have been on since joining De Souza 4 (or so) years ago. Both have demonstrated a huge boost in self confidence and have learnt life long skills, with some great friendships along the way!

I recall a recent tournament, where prior to attending our eldest son was having some self confidence issues, we were worried about him. After discussions with the De Souza team they believed he could do well and encouraged us to enter him.

On the day of the tournament, he was nervous and repeatedly asked not to go, as he doubted himself. However, once we got there, his attitude changed and Alex gave him some fantastic motivational words. He was moved to a higher weight category, and he won his fight, winning gold!

Since this point, he has been a new boy. His confidence has grown and he is performing better in school and other sporting activities. We attribute this solely to that day, as the transformation was overnight, but in truth it was combined with all the amazing training and compassion that led to him winning.

With the continued training, support and care of the De Souza team there will hopefully be more gold to come for both our sons!

***Parents of Arthur, 10 & Otto, 12***

From an early age, my little girl was very sporty. Gymnastics, dancing, football etc. I felt that I should introduce her to a combat sport as she got older.

Something that would help protect her through her life and to compete in competition. I waited until she was 8 years old and took her to Brazilian Jiu-Jitsu. She took to it well and enjoyed it.

She is now 11 years old, with a grey belt and 3 gold medals. She has become a very confident strong little girl, with more belief and control in herself.

She has made great friendships and loves her time at the Dojo. Jiu-Jitsu has and will continue to help her grow into the woman she will become.

***Parents of Maya, 11***

We can see the difference in Kamronbek now.
He is more confident and self-disciplined.

Also after Jiu-Jitsu lessons he has
got a great appetite :-).

He loves it and he says it's so much fun!

**_Parents of Kamronbek, 5_**

Since Sonny has started training in Brazilian Jiu-Jitsu we have noticed many positive changes in him, he can control his temper better, he's getting fitter, stronger and he has grown in confidence now he is able to do more moves and understand how the art of Brazilian Jiu-Jitsu works.

Alex has a good mix of patience and discipline sprinkled with a good sense of humour. Would recommend to any families.

*Parents of Sonny, 8*

Brazilian Jiu-Jitsu has played a very important part in our lives as a family over the last few years and we couldn't imagine life without it.

It has really helped with Honey and Louis confidence and self esteem.

I think it has also really helped them both to understand and show a level of respect for themselves and other people.

*Parents of Honey-Mai, 5 & Louis, 11*

Brazilian Jiu-Jitsu has benefitted my son by giving him discipline and focus added in with learning a new skill.

With the skills he is learning his confidence has sky rocketed and also his ability to listen and understand directions.

*Parents of Sonny, 6*

*Maya with Alex De Souza*

*Drawing by our student Daniel of our dojo where the children train*

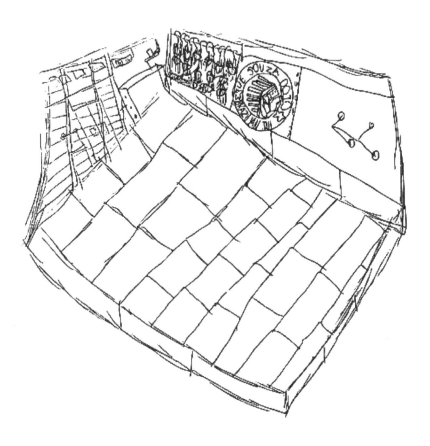

# OSS

Printed in Great Britain
by Amazon

47320467R00066